EXPERIMENTS WITH GRAVITY

A TRUE BOOK®

by

Salvatore Tocci

Children's Press®

A Division of Scholastic Inc.

New York Toronto London Auckland Sydney
Mexico City New Delhi Hong Kong
Danbury, Connecticut

Reading Consultant
Nanci R. Vargus, Ed.D
Primary Multiage Teacher
Decatur Township Schools
Indianapolis, Indiana

Science Consultant
Robert Gardner

The photo on the cover is a roller coaster speeding down the track. The photo on the title page shows a skydiver in free fall.

The author and publisher are not responsible for injuries or accidents that occur during or from any experiments. Experiments should be conducted in the presence of or with the help of an adult. Any instructions of the experiments that require the use of sharp, hot, or other unsafe items should be conducted by or with the help of an adult.

Library of Congress Cataloging-in-Publication Data

Tocci, Salvatore.
Experiments with gravity / Salvatore Tocci
    p. cm. — (A True Book)
   Includes biographical references and index.
   Summary: Experiments introduce and explain the concept of gravity.
   ISBN 0-516-22513-8 (lib. bdg.)   0-516-29364-8 (pbk)
   1. Gravity—Experiments—Juvenile literature. [1. Gravity—Experiments.
2. Experiments.] I. Title. II. Series.
QC178 .T63 2002
531'.5'078—dc21

2001004943

Contents

These astronauts are floating in zero gravity on the space shuttle.

Can Something Weigh Nothing?

Do you know someone who is trying to lose **weight**? Many people try to lose weight by going on a diet. Some people follow a diet that includes foods with little or no fat. Other people may follow a diet where they eat any kind

5

of food, but limit how much they eat.

Perhaps the person you know is trying to lose weight by exercising. Exercising uses up the energy from food that is stored in the body. People who exercise to lose weight may jog, play tennis, or walk on a treadmill several times a week.

Astronauts can lose weight without dieting or exercising.

All they must do is get away from Earth. Whenever they are traveling in space, astronauts weigh much less than they do on Earth. In fact, once astronauts leave Earth's **atmosphere**—the layer of air around the Earth—they feel as if they weigh almost nothing. What these astronauts have done is gotten away from something called **gravity**.

What Is Gravity?

Why does a ball you throw into the air always come back down? The ball comes back down because of gravity. Gravity is a force that pulls on an object. All objects pull on one another because of gravity. For example, the ball's gravity pulls on Earth. In turn, Earth's gravity pulls on

Why does the ball always come back down?

the ball. Both the ball and
Earth pull on each other with
the same force.

However, Earth is much
larger than the ball. Because it

9

is much smaller, the ball moves much more than Earth. So when you throw the ball into the air, both the ball and Earth move toward each other. Because of it huge size, Earth hardly moves at all. Because of its very small size, the ball moves very easily. As a result, the ball in the air is quickly pulled back down by Earth's gravity. But does Earth's gravity always pull an object in the same direction?

Hanging Down

You will need:
- scissors
- ruler
- string
- paper clip
- masking tape
- piece of white paper
- table
- pencil
- two books of equal height

Cut a 12-inch (30 cm) length of string. Tie the paper clip to one end of the string. Tie the other end of the string around the middle of the ruler. Tape the string so that it cannot slide along the ruler. Place the piece of paper on the table. Stand the books upright on the paper about 10 in. (25 cm) apart. Place the ends of the ruler on the tops of the book. Mark the spot on the paper

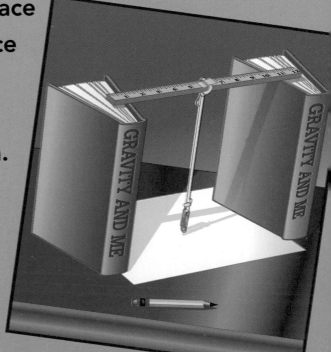

where the paper clip points. Hold one end of the ruler about 6 inches above the top of the book. Does the paper clip point to the same spot as it did before?

Try tilting the ruler from its other end. Notice that the paper clip points to different spots on the paper. The paper clip always hangs straight down, no matter how you tilt the ruler. Earth's gravity is a force that always pulls objects downward so that they fall toward the center of Earth. But does Earth's gravity make a heavier object fall faster than a lighter object?

Earth's gravity always pulls objects toward its center.

Experiment 2

Timing the Drop

You will need:
- newspaper
- chair
- a helper
- two lemons
- grape

Spread the newspaper on the floor in front of the chair. Ask someone to stand on the chair and hold a lemon in each hand. Tell your friend to extend his or her arms straight out so that his or her hands are over the newspaper. Make sure that both lemons are the same height above the floor. Lay on the floor so that your eyes are almost level with the newspaper. Tell the person to let go of both lemons at the same time. Do both lemons hit the floor at the same time?

You probably were not surprised to see that both lemons landed on the floor at the same time. After all, both are almost the same size. What happens when you repeat this experiment using a grape in place of one of the lemons? Does the lemon, which is larger and heavier, fall faster than the grape?

You probably were surprised to see that both the lemon and the grape hit the floor at the same time. Earth's gravity pulls all objects downward at the same speed, no matter how large or small they are.

Earth's gravity pulls an object downward with a certain amount of force. This amount of force is called weight. You can find the weight of an object by placing it on a scale.

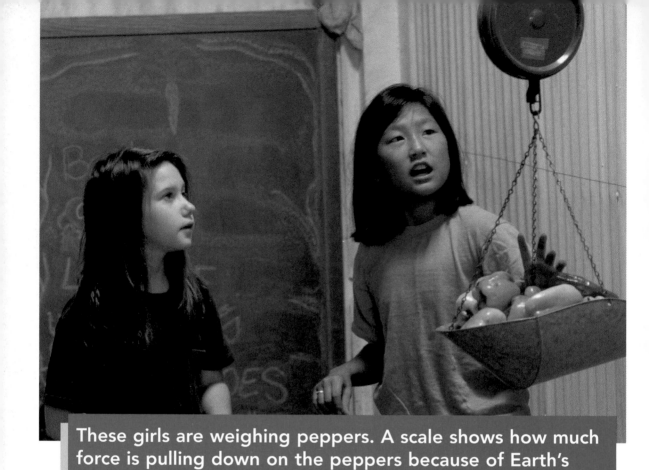

These girls are weighing peppers. A scale shows how much force is pulling down on the peppers because of Earth's gravity. Weight is a measurement of this force.

You are probably familiar with scales that measure weight in ounces or pounds. See how simple it is to make your own scale.

Weighing Objects

You will need:
- masking tape
- coiled spring toy
- door frame
- paper cup
- pencil
- scissors
- string
- white paper
- quarter
- small objects
- ruler

Tape one end of the coiled spring toy to the top of the door frame about $\frac{1}{2}$ in. ($1\frac{1}{4}$ cm) away from one side. Draw an arrow under the rim of the paper cup so that it points to the side. Use the pencil to punch two holes on opposite sides of the paper cup. Push a piece of string through the holes in the cup and tie it in a loop. Hang the string on the bottom loop of the

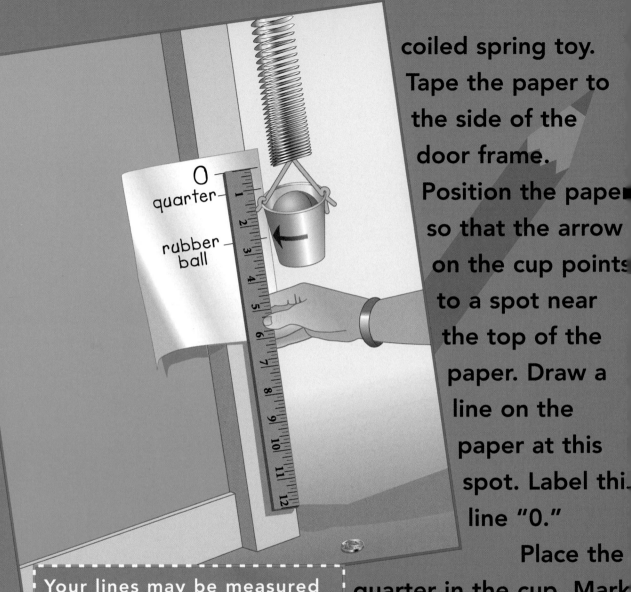

coiled spring toy. Tape the paper to the side of the door frame. Position the paper so that the arrow on the cup points to a spot near the top of the paper. Draw a line on the paper at this spot. Label this line "0."

Place the quarter in the cup. Mark the paper to show where the arrow on the

Your lines may be measured in fractions of inches. In this case, if a line is $2\frac{1}{2}$ inches away from the 0 line, then the object is $2\frac{1}{2}$ times heavier than the quarter.

cup now points. Draw a line and label it "quarter." Remove the coin from the cup. Place another small object in the cup. Again mark the paper to show where the arrow points and draw a line. Label this line with the name of the object you put in the cup. Remove the object and repeat the procedure with all the small objects you have.

Measure the distance from the line labeled "0" to each of the other lines. Suppose the line labeled "quarter" was 1 in. ($2\frac{1}{2}$ cm) from the "0" line. Suppose another object made a line 2 in. ($7\frac{1}{4}$ cm) away from the "0" line. Then this object is twice as heavy as the quarter. If a line is 4 in. (10 cm) away from the "0" line, then the object in the cup is four times heavier than the quarter.

The father has more mass and therefore weighs more than the child.

The weight of an object depends on two things. One is how much **mass**, or stuff, the object has. The more mass it has, the more the object weighs.

The other thing that affects weight is gravity. The stronger the pull by Earth's gravity, the more the object weighs. If the object is far enough away from Earth, then Earth's gravity would not pull on the object. If the object were not being pulled by gravity, then it would not weigh anything. However, the object would still have mass.

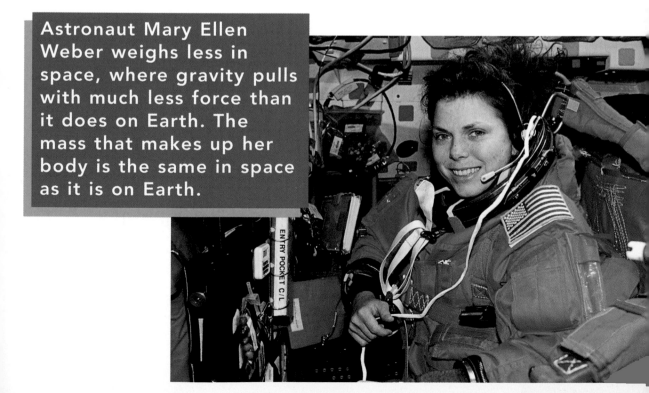

Astronaut Mary Ellen Weber weighs less in space, where gravity pulls with much less force than it does on Earth. The mass that makes up her body is the same in space as it is on Earth.

What Can Gravity Do?

Gravity is a force of attraction between two objects. Earth's gravity pulls on an object, giving it weight. Earth's gravity also pulls on objects so that they fall toward the center of Earth. Learn how Earth's gravity can make an object swing back and forth.

Experiment 4

Swinging Back and Forth

You will need:
- measuring tape
- scissors
- string
- metal nut
- masking tape
- door frame
- clock or watch with a second hand

Cut a 4-foot (1.2-meter) length of string. Tie the nut to one end. Tape the other end of the string to the top of the door frame. Raise the nut a little to one side and drop it so that it starts swinging. Time how long it takes for the nut to swing ten times from one side to the other and then back.

Just release the nut to start it swinging. Do not push it.

Now raise the nut higher to one side and drop it to start it swinging. Again time how long it takes for the nut to swing back and forth ten times. Notice that the nut makes a wider swing when you start it swinging from a greater height. But does it take more time to swing back and forth ten times than it did when you started it swinging from a lower height? You should discover that it takes the same amount of time to complete ten swings, no matter where it starts swinging.

What you have made is a **pendulum**. A pendulum is a mass that is held in the air

A grandfather clock uses a pendulum. The pendulum always takes the same amount of time to make one complete swing.

and that swings back and forth. The nut is the mass held in the air by the string. When you raise the nut, gravity pulls it down as soon as you release it. When it reaches the bottom of its swing, the nut begins to move upward. As the nut swings upward, gravity is still pulling it down. With gravity pulling on it, the nut can go no higher than the height you released it. At this point, the nut stops. Gravity then causes the nut to swing back. The width of each swing gets smaller and smaller until the pendulum finally stops. What else can gravity do besides make a pendulum swing back and forth?

Gravity is always pulling the nut toward Earth. Gravity helps keep the nut swinging back and forth.

Experiment 5

Keeping Time

You will need:
- pitcher
- empty 2-liter plastic bottle
- scissors
- masking tape
- marker
- straight pin
- paper cup
- an adult helper
- clock or watch with a second hand

Fill the pitcher with water. Ask an adult to cut the top off the bottle. Stick a piece of masking tape on the side of the bottle. Draw a line across the tape near the bottom. Fill the bottle with water up to this mark.

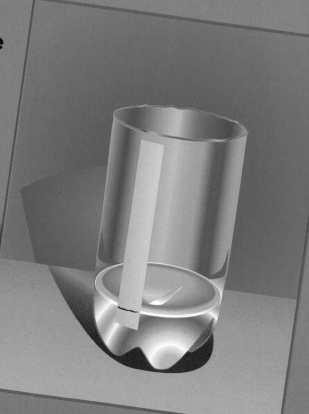

Use the pin to poke a tiny hole on the side of the paper cup near the bottom. Ask the adult to hold the cup so that its bottom is inside the bottle, just below the top. Have the adult place a finger over the hole in the cup. Then fill the cup with water from the pitcher.

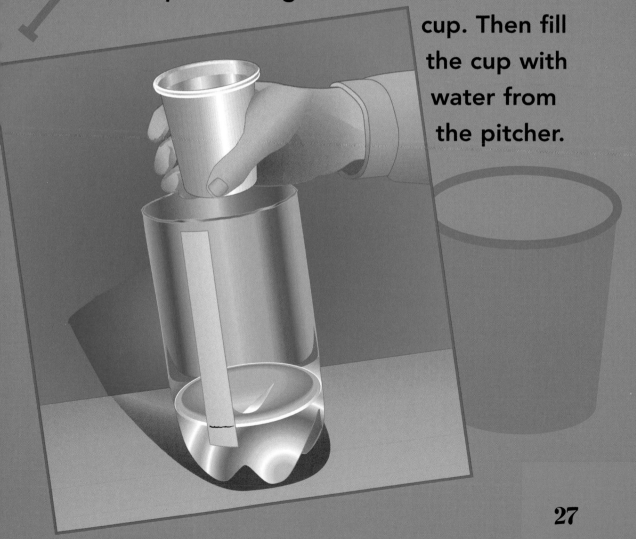

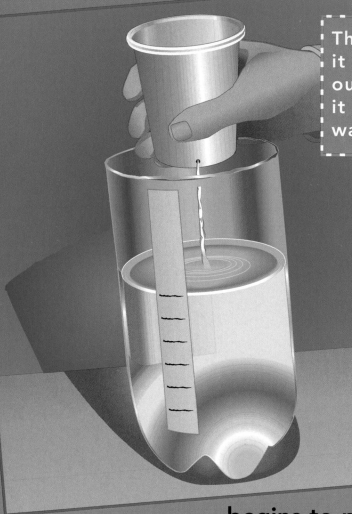

These lines mark the minutes it took for the water to flow out of the cup. Notice that it took 5 minutes for the water to reach the top mark.

While you keep track of time, have the adult remove his or her finger from the hole. Start timing as soon as water begins to pour out of the cup. Ask the adult to use the pitcher to keep the cup filled with water. Every minute, mark the water level on the tape with a line and number. Do this for five minutes.

Empty the bottle. Fill it with water to the first mark. Then repeat the experiment, but see if you can tell when a minute has passed just by looking at the bottle. Gravity will pull the water so that it falls at the same speed every time. What you have made is a clock that works by gravity. Learn what else works by gravity.

Have you ever played a game in which you used a timer like this?

Experiment 6

Taking a Ride

You will need:
- $\frac{1}{4}$-in. ($\frac{3}{4}$ cm) piece of wood about 6 in. (15 cm) wide and 12 in. (30 cm) long
- three books, each with about the same number of pages
- toy car
- masking tape

Make a ramp by setting one end of the piece of wood on a book. Hold the toy car at the top of the ramp and then release it. Begin counting as soon as you release the car. How many counts does it take for the car to reach the end of the ramp? Use tape to mark the spot where the car stops.

Add another book so that the ramp is steeper. Release the car again. How many counts does it take this time for the car to reach the end of the ramp? Does the car travel farther this time? Repeat this

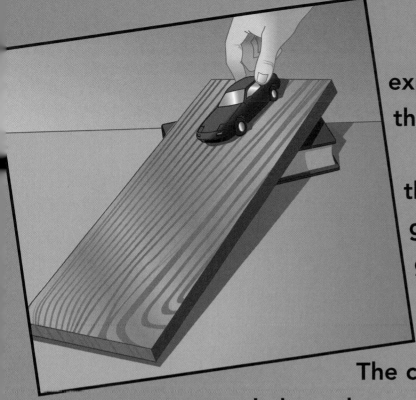

experiment with a third book.

The higher the car, the faster gravity makes it go and the farther gravity makes it travel. The cars on a roller coaster speed along the track because of gravity. These cars have no motors. They are pulled to the top of a steep hill and then released. Gravity pulls them down. The higher and steeper the hill, the faster and farther they will travel along the track.

Can You Defy Gravity?

Gravity pulls everything toward the center of Earth. Is there any way to defy or resist Earth's gravity? One way is to travel deep into space, where there is no pull by Earth's gravity. Is there some way, however, to defy gravity right here on Earth?

Rolling Uphill

You will need:
- two rubber bands
- round lid without a lip (like one from a jar of peanut butter)
- three marbles
- masking tape
- piece of cardboard

Space the rubber bands evenly around the lid. Use the tape to stick the marbles to the inside of the lid. Fold one edge of the cardboard and set the folded edge on the floor to make a ramp. Stand the lid on its edge at the bottom of the ramp.

Think of the lid as the face of a clock. Set the marbles so that they are at the 2:00 position.

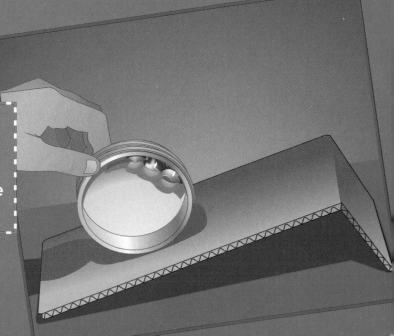

Make sure that the marbles are placed so that they face up the ramp. Let go of the lid and watch what happens.

Normally, things roll down a hill because of gravity. The lid seems to defy gravity by rolling up the hill. To understand why this happens, you need to know how gravity pulls on an object. Gravity always pulls at just one point on an object. This point is called the center of gravity.

The center of gravity of some objects, like the lid with marbles, is the heaviest part.

The marbles cannot fall straight down because they are taped to the lid. So they can only fall down by moving forward. This causes the lid to roll uphill.

The lid's center of gravity, then, is the spot where the marbles are. Because the marbles are near the top, gravity pulls downward on this spot. This causes the lid to roll forward and move slowly up the hill. The lid is not defying gravity. It rolls the way it does because of gravity.

Objects traveling in space, like the space shuttle and satellites, seem to defy gravity. After all, they are close enough to Earth to be pulled by its gravity. Then why don't they come crashing back down to Earth?

Experiment 8

Circling Earth

You will need:
- round lid without a lip (like one from a jar of peanut butter)
- table or other flat surface
- scissors
- marble

Set the lid upside down on the table. Place the marble against the rim of the lid. Push the marble so that it starts rolling around the rim. The marble acts like a satellite that keeps circling Earth. As long as the marble keeps moving fast enough, it will continue to go around in circles. But once the marble slows down, it will stop going around in circles. If a satellite

36

is not traveling fast
enough, it, too, will stop circling Earth.
Instead, the satellite will be pulled by gravity and
crash back to Earth.

   While it is circling the Earth, gravity keeps the
satellite from flying off into space. To see what
would happen to a satellite if there were no
gravity, cut away several inches of the lid's edge.

Place the marble near the area you cut. Push the marble to start it rolling around the rim. What happens to the marble when it reaches the opening in the lid? Without a rim to hold it in, the marble should shoot straight out, away from the lid. Without gravity to pull in it, a satellite would fly straight out into space.

Gravity is a force that pulls on all objects. Two objects move toward each other because of gravity. Earth's gravity pulls objects toward its center. The pull of Earth's gravity gives an object its weight. An object has weight unless it leaves Earth's atmosphere and escapes Earth's gravity.

Fun With Gravity

Now that you've learned a few things about gravity, here's a fun experiment to try. Challenge your friends to balance a piece of cardboard on one finger. They won't be able to do it. But you will because you know where its center of gravity is.

Balancing Act

You will need:
- scissors
- cardboard
- nail
- string
- modeling clay
- paper clip
- tape
- table
- pencil
- ruler

Cut out an uneven shape from the cardboard. Use the nail to make a small hole at opposite edges of the cut-out figure. Cut a piece of string that is long enough to stretch across the figure. Tie a loop in one end of the string. Tie the other end of the string around a small ball of clay.

Unbend the paper clip to make a hook. Tape it to

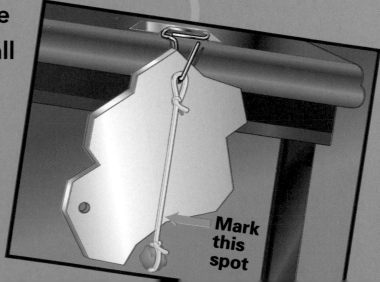

Mark this spot

Pencil line

Spot you marked

the edge of the table. Hang the cardboard figure on the hook. Make sure that it swings freely.

Next, hang the loop of the string on the hook.

Wait until the string stops swinging. Then, use the pencil to mark the spot where the string crosses the edge of the cardboard figure. Remove the figure from the hook. Draw a line from the spot you marked to the hole where it hung on the hook.

Now, hang the figure on the hook using the other hole. Again, hang the string by the loop.

Mark another spot on the figure where the string now crosses the edge of the figure. Remove the figure from the hook. Draw a second line on the figure from this spot to the hole where it hung on the hook. The point where the two lines cross is the figure's center of gravity. You can now balance the cardboard by placing your finger at its center of gravity.

Ask a friend to try to balance the cardboard on one finger. But don't tell how to find the figure's center of gravity. You'll see how much trouble your friend will have trying to balance the figure.

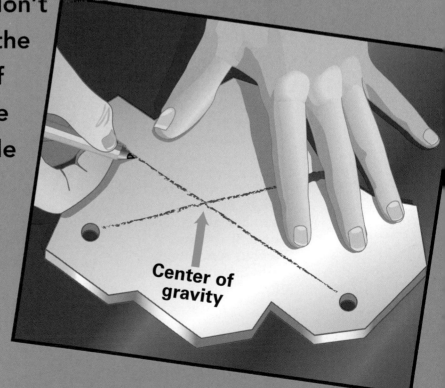

Center of gravity

To Find Out More

If you would like to learn more about gravity, check out these additional resources.

 **Books**

Ardley, Neil. **The Science Book of Gravity.** Harcourt Brace Jovanovich, 1992.

Stringer, John. **The Science of Gravity.** Raintree/ Steck Vaughn, 2000.

Thompson, Kim. M. And Karen M. Hilderbrand. **I'd Like to Be an Astronaut: Learning About Gravity, Space Travel and Famous Astronauts.** Twins Sisters Productions, 1996.

White, Larry. **Gravity: Simple Experiments for Young Scientists.** Millbrook Press, 1996.

Wiese, Jim. **Cosmic Science: Over 40 Gravity-Defying, Earth-Orbiting, Space-Cruising Activities for Kids.** John Wiley & Sons, 1997.